I0541298

Ant to Zinnia
Nature's ABCs

Hyda Maria Dougherty

Tribal Eye Productions
Santa Ynez, CA

Ant to Zinnia: Nature's ABCs

© 2014 Hyda Maria Dougherty

All Rights Reserved. No portion of this book may be reproduced by any means, except for brief quotations in reviews, without written permission from the publisher.

Printed in the USA

Tribal Eye Productions
P.O. Box 1123 / Santa Ynez, CA 93460
TribalEyePro@gmail.com

ISBN: 979-8-9887862-6-9

Acknowledgments

I am most grateful to my mother, Ms. Laura Dougherty (1903-1992) She taught and inspired thousands of children to learn how to read and write. Ms. Dougherty's dedication, compassion and creativity have been my motivation to offer these Nature's ABC books.

Many thanks to my grown children and hundreds of other children that I have taught and continue to teach as they help to keep me engaged, informed, and they are my best editors.

A special thanks to family: Larry, Marty and Kevin Parcell who have always been there when I needed them the most as have Manuel and Elizabeth Romero. I am also grateful to Marisela Romero for her interest and support of the ABC books both as a professional and as a parent.

My gratitude extends to Anna Marie Houser and to Phillip Haozous who have believed in me every step of the way and provided valuable feedback and innumerable resources.

My sincere appreciation to Gary Robinson, the publisher. Many thanks for the patience and guidance of the proofreaders: Michelle Martinez, Lauren Roberts and Shawn Newell.

I would like to recognize a few of the many friends that have contributed in so many ways: Tari Woods for a quiet, restorative place to stay for inspiration. Evelyn Jones who provides a serene place at her ranch for me to write and paint. Sylvia Chavez, an educator with valuable insights. Concha Allen, Patricia Sigala and Madi Sato influence my integration of music, art, and dance for children.

The Author

ANT to ZINNIA NATURE'S ABC's

This book is an introduction and an invitation for children to explore the natural world around them. It is a back to basics sensorial approach to learning. It is fun and inspires a desire to learn. Children are interested in the world around them. This book builds upon their curiosity. It has an easy-to-follow format that can be used in a variety of ways.

Each letter has a word and a verse that goes with it. One may introduce the ABC book by having the child look at the pictures and talk about them. At first the verses can be read to children and eventually they are able to recognize the letters, sound out the words and read the verses themselves.

It is very helpful to also obtain the *Ant to Zinnia Nature Activities* book. This book goes hand in hand with this *Ant to Zinnia Nature's ABC* book and integrates art, music and movement in the lessons. It is designed for and successfully used to teach early childhood education, special education and English as a second language students. Both books are easily adapted to a child's learning style and interest giving them a solid foundation in reading and writing while exploring and learning to appreciate the wonders of nature.

I dedicate this body of work to my mother, Laura Dougherty, fondly known as Mamacita, who dedicated her life to serving children and who has inspired many including me, to build upon our talents and interests. Her memory lives in the hearts of all the children she taught. I am grateful to all the people who have made it possible to offer this Literacy Arts program for children.

Hyda Maria Dougherty

Ant ate a bit of an apple. She gave the rest to her family.

ANT

B b

"Baa, baa", bleated baby lamb as she chased a blue butterfly from flower to flower.

BAA

Cat likes to sleep
in the sun all day
then she likes to run
and play all night.

CAT

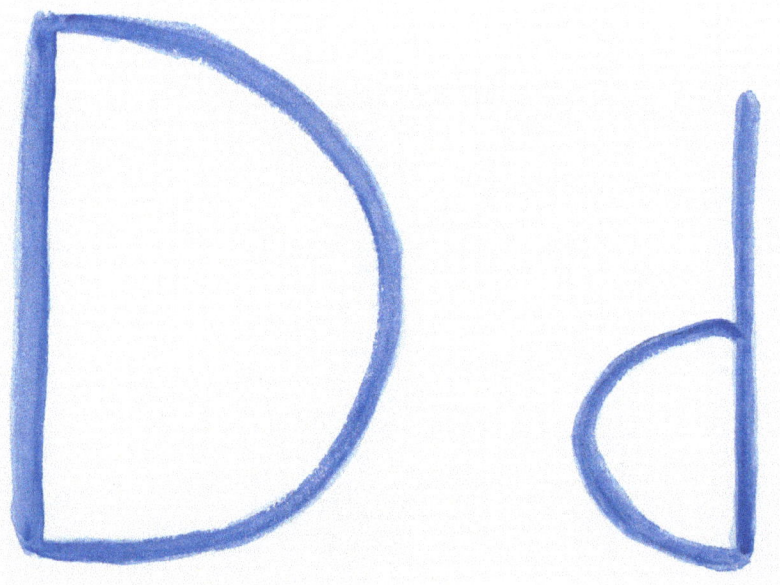

Drake is a daddy duck.
He lives on a lake with
his mate Dixie and their
three baby ducklings.

DUCK

Eagle eggs shake
and their shells break
as the baby eaglets
are born.

EGG

Frogs frolic in the rain. They leap over rocks and logs to splash in the puddles.

FROG

Go green as a bamboo
tree that sways to and fro
in the breeze. See it grows
tall under the sun and rain.

Our hens feathers are
soft brown with red, orange
and yellow highlights.

HEN

Inuit Indians build houses made with ice blocks called igloos.

IGLOO

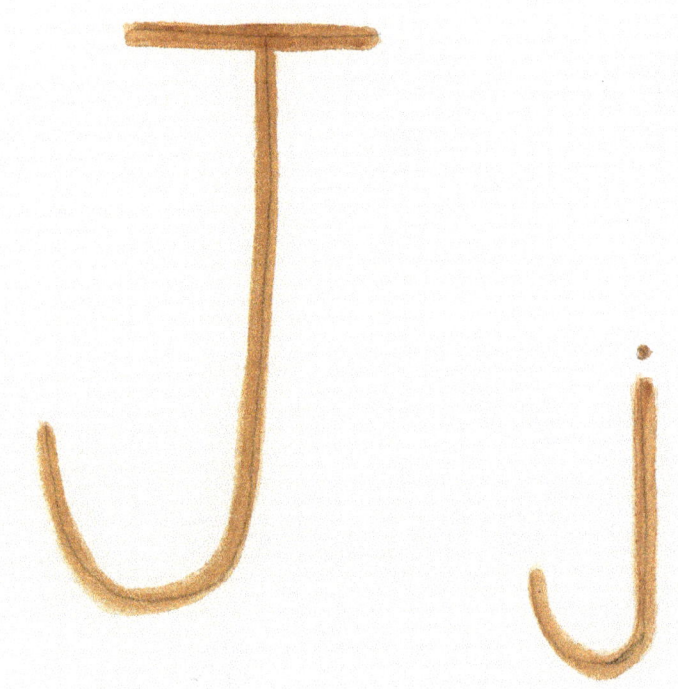

Jays squawk loudly to let each other know if an animal of prey like a cat is nearby.

JAY

K k

The March wind blows our kite ever so high it touches blue skies.

I like lollipops that taste like fruit. My favorite flavors are cherry and grape.

LOLLIPOP

M m

Monkeys like to climb
and swing in the trees
just like me.

MONKEY

Birds gather leaves, grass and twigs to build a safe and warm nest for their eggs and baby chicks.

NEST

Octopus lives in the sea and she changes color like a chameleon.

OCTOPUS

The pink pig and her
baby piglet like to eat
pumpkins from our garden.

PIG

Many quail follow
Hale as he feeds them
seeds from his yellow
pail.

QUAIL

R r

Sing a song about
a rabbit with a pink nose
who goes hop, hop, hop!

RABBIT

Snake slithers in the
grass and sun bathes
sleepily on the rocks.

SNAKE

Timothy and Tina
turtle take a slow walk
down to the lake.

TURTLE

Up, Up, go our
umbrellas come
rain or sun shine.

UMBRELLA

We have violets, daisies
and roses in a vase for
Valentines day.

VASE

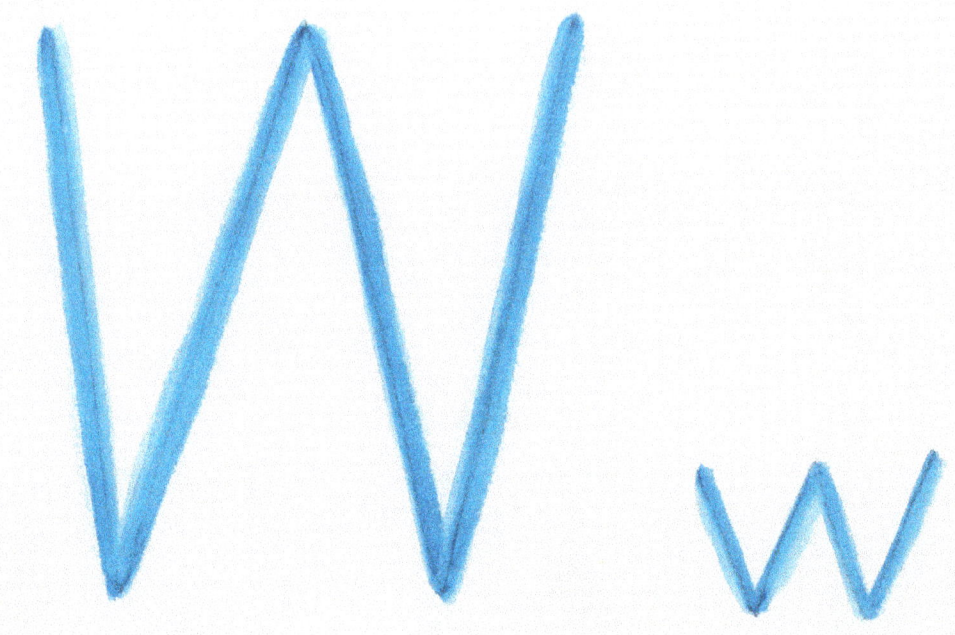

Whales are the largest animals in the world. They are fast swimmers and tail slapping songsters.

WHALE

I am an x-ray fish.
Light shines through me
so you can see my bones.

X-RAY

Round and round
up and down on a
string go our yo-yo's.

YO YO

Bees buzz busily as they zig-zig from zinnia to zinnia flowers.

YO YO

Z z

Bees buzz busily as they zig-zig from zinnia to zinnia flowers.

ZINNIA

Hyda Maria Dougherty is a native New Mexican and a lifelong resident of Santa Fe. Through both the development of early-learning curriculum and direct instruction, she has been a reliable advocate of children's literacy through the course of her career.

Drawing inspiration from nature and from the stories, songs, and dances of the Indigenous cultures of the region. Ms. Dougherty has created this fun and engaging literacy-focused learning tool. With, *"Ant to Zinnia Nature's ABC's"* and its companion book, *"Ant to Zinnia Nature Activities"* in hand, children will be better equipped to begin—and share—their own imaginative adventures through literature and its respective arts.

The *"Ant to Zinnia"* set is a must-have for the beginning or challenged reader: a playful educational experience for the child; and a solid, trustworthy choice for grown-up curators of the young reader's library.

Photo by Daniel Quat / Bio written by Rosemary Diaz

© Hyda Maria Dougherty

www.ingramcontent.com/pod-product-compliance
Lightning Source LLC
Chambersburg PA
CBHW041541120626
46551CB00019B/2794